THIS WALKER BOOK BELONGS TO:

_____

_____

_____

_____

Under the GROUND

Illustrated by **Sally Hobson**

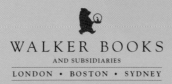

WALKER BOOKS

AND SUBSIDIARIES

LONDON · BOSTON · SYDNEY

Whose silver **train** is this?

twitch twitch

Whose
fluffy
babies
are these?

Mine!

said the **rabbit**.

I live with my babies in
a safe, cosy home called
a nursery burrow.

Whose spiky **wheel** is this?

My spiky wheel
spins round to
cut through
the coal.

said the
coal miner.

said the **worm**.

My wriggly body is great
for tunnelling through
the soil.

Whose wriggly **body** is this?

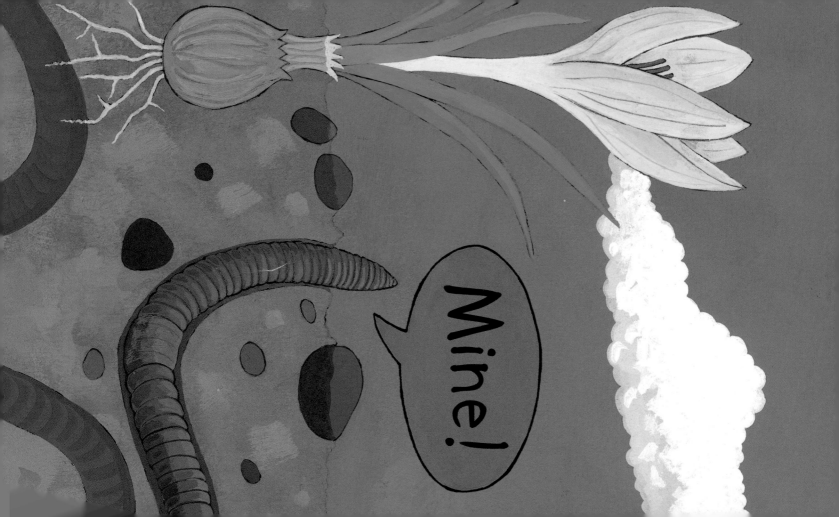

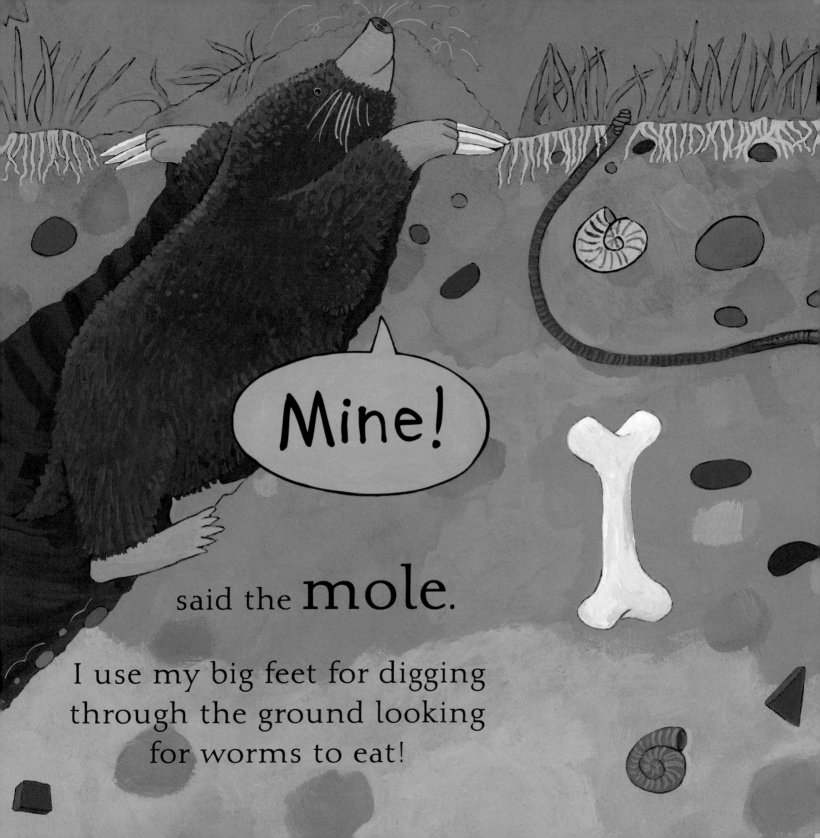

Here we are, under the ground.
Can you find the coal miner,
the rabbits, the train driver,
the mole, the ants and
the worms?

Whose
black
legs
are these?

Whose big feet are these?

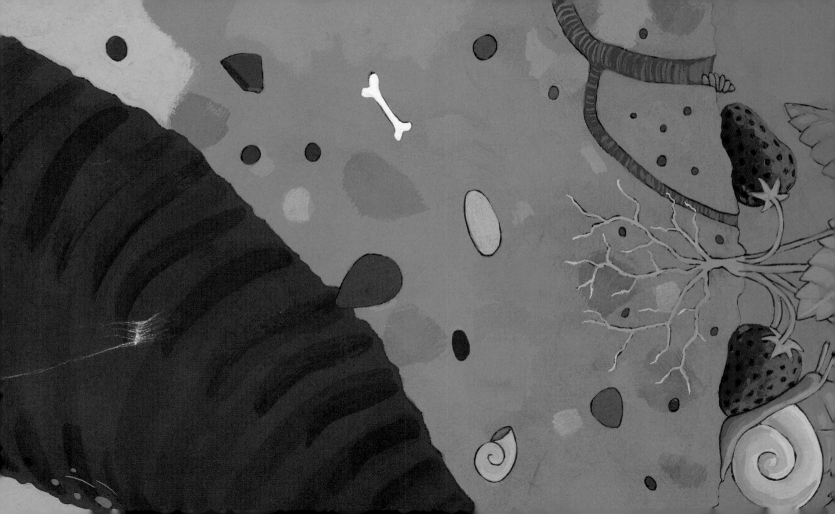

First published 2001 by Walker Books Ltd
87 Vauxhall Walk, London SE11 5HJ

This edition published 2002

2   4   6   8   10   9   7   5   3   1

Series concept by Louise Jackson

Words by Paul Harrison and Louise Jackson

Designed by Justin Hunt

Wildlife consultant: Martin Jenkins

This book has been typeset in Calligraphic

Printed in Hong Kong

British Library Cataloguing in Publication Data:
a catalogue record for this book is available
from the British Library

ISBN 0-7445-7751-9

Walker Flip-flap Facts

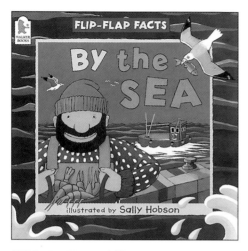

ISBN 0-7445-7748-9 (pb)

ISBN 0-7445-7749-7 (pb)

ISBN 0-7445-7750-0 (pb)

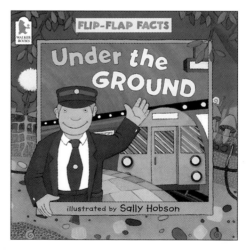

ISBN 0-7445-7751-9 (pb)

Collect them all!